When You Can't See a Way

When You Can't See a Way

Theta Burke

Delafield Press   Suttons Bay, Michigan 49682

ISBN: 0-916872-08-4
Library of Congress Catalog Card Number: 85-072772
Printed in the United States of America

The soul would say

Yes, I am your pain
    but I am also
your peace and your power
Know always
that I am aware and able.

When You Can't See a Way

through your dark

understandings illumine

the light is within

through your dark

1.

When you can't see a way
through the lonely pain
and you long sometimes
    for the courage to die
There's a light in your night
a hand reaching out
and a heart that understands why.

2.

Weary, just weary
of trying
of hoping for some brighter day
when all the steps
I have taken
don't seem to lead to the way

Heartache
and heartbreak
are mostly what's felt
a yearning and reaching
rejection of self

What good am I
life just questions why
no reason for living
afraid yet to die.

3.

I see from whence
you've journeyed
the struggling pain you've known
I feel the lonely heartbreak
when a treasured dream seems gone

I cannot know the reasons
for its delay in time
but I know the author
        of that dream
has a purpose still in mind.

4.

Steps I take again
      uncertain
      tentative
      doubting
toward what I hope
is the right direction

You cannot know
the lonely despair
      and isolation I feel
when your concern
      is expressed
by critical judgment
of my efforts.

5.

Too weak and too weary
to struggle
that's how it feels right now
Can't see a way
it could ever be better
it's beyond my believing a "how"

The darkness now
seems all there is
the light feels gone from my soul
Will the sun ever change
this darkest of nights
this bleakness of being alone.

6.

An image projected
but not yet connected
how will I ever feel real
Speaking a theory
        but lacking in practice
too many parts to conceal

Living in shadows
afraid of the light
can ever the Self be revealed
Too frightened and crying
        uncertain, denying
a life unready to live

Oh, where is the reason
to risk who I am
to let it be *felt* by me
Afraid of rejection
        by open expression
to others — or even to me.

7.

He takes to the highways
and by-ways
when peace has gone from his soul
A heart that is heavy
and aching
too heavy — too heavy the load

Too many trials beset him
without a way he can see
He has given himself
         in ways that he can
but his loving
they do not perceive.

8.

To have to learn
to walk the way
alone without you here
seems much too hard and lonely
more, it seems, than I can bear

The part of me
that's gone with you
makes numb the other part
as I walk alone with silent tears
a body without a heart

They say that time
can heal the pain
and I know it's probably so
but Time's not now
the pain is deep
and I can't see the way to go

The road ahead
seems much too far
when I must walk alone
with all the pain
without you here
to give to life its song

How long will memories
make me cry
when will I cease
to want to die

How long for time
to heal my pain
to feel the joy
of life again.

9.

The overwhelming flood
         of sorrow and despair
has left me awash
on the shore

Letting the sadness
         seep in
as deeply as it can
Feeling my heart wrench
with the pain
         of my loss
is all I can do now.

10.

Many have succeeded
and many more have contemplated
    ending their lives
And always we ask the question
why — why

I think it would seem
all hope would be gone
with a feeling so terribly
    so terribly alone
Do we know
Have we ever felt so
Not truly
We never took that road

But most of us
have walked the path
that could have led to such an act
Somewhere someone gave us hope
and we somehow traveled back

Would that we'd remember
despair that can't be told
and search the way with one who needs
a way that points to hope.

11.

We walked the road
so many years — together
I never thought
you'd go away — no, never

But a heart can't know
what time will show

Will my heart ache forever?

12.

My mother died
And they thought
    I would be relieved
that her suffering had ended

But they could not know
that her death left still unanswered
    my eternal question
Did she love me?

13.

A sadness settles over
       weighting my soul
broken in too many pieces
to put together now
And I am weary
       with the struggle

Perhaps the stillness
can speak

I do not want to hear
voices.

14.

Each time
you don't believe in me
I shut away from you
      a part of myself

What will I do
      when there's no part to share
with you?

15.

Oftimes
when I speak my despair
I do not want you
      to offer solutions

My heart needs only
your listening care.

16.

So many, many see and say
it's up to me to find my way
but oft I need a helping hand
a soul to care and understand

The pain is hidden deep inside
as are the tears that I can't cry
and what another cannot see
can he believe that it could be

So I go along my lonely way
feeling what I cannot say
making the outside look okay
though the inside fear won't go away

If I were able
to let you know
that deepest pain I cannot show
perhaps I'd know a healing balm
a peaceful heart, an inner calm.

17.

I want you and need you
he said to her
And I hate you for that
and I hate me

When I was ten
my father died
       and my mother turned away
When she could not love me
I rejected all women

If I can allow
my loving and needing you
perhaps I can learn
       not to hate you or me.

18.

The outside has learned
to look strong and sure
and speaks what I hope
        can someday be *felt*

Inside
there is still a lonely child
fragile and uncertain
        seeking support
spoken by your understanding.

19.

The acorn
becomes a sapling
The sapling
becomes a tree

Do you think the acorn
can see ahead
to what it is
        that it will be?

20.

Unspent portions
    of thy soul
Dreams within thee
yet untold

All this and more
eternity holds.

understandings illumine

21.

The seed
could not believe
    that the dark earth
could be good for it

How could it know
    the transformation
the soil's nutrients
would accomplish
    in its being?

22.

They speak of all
the joys of love
the happiness it brings
but somewhere in the telling
they forgot to tell its pain

Love builds a nest
and lines it
with a downy gossamer
where rest its tend'rest moments
which evermore endure

But then comes Pain
o'erwhelming
and making all feel lost
where is the joy — the happiness
my soul feels naught but loss

Ah, yes, speaks Pain
I come with love
I come to add the strength
for going deeper in your soul
than you might ever think

Resist not either feeling
they must walk hand in hand

To know the depth
of love you'd have
its pain your heart
must understand

23.

One who has walked farther
        along the road of love
must at times retrace his steps
to walk with one
        in his early learning

It may not be enough
        that he stand and beckon
with extended arms.

24.

So-called greed
is but the feeling of need
attempting to be fulfilled

An awareness and appreciation
of our inner unfolding
        is that which allows
our poverty to become plenty.

25.

The process of accepting
       what is or has been
is not a passive or compliant way

It is a quiet, positive energy
       which absorbs realities
and allows for their processing
by our understanding
so that they become a resource
       rather than a restraint.

26.

Walk slowly and gently, my friend,
into the house of my Being

Discover first in me
      a strength
and converse with that part
so that I may develop the security
      to share that
which feels less strong.

27.

When you did not take a way
you wish that you had gone
think of the reason you made the choice
don't just say you were wrong

For we decide just what to do
from a particular point of view
from where we are
at a given time
and it cannot be
      a different view

And when we make
the same mistake
and think we should have learned
Just give things time
to grow inside
so the outer can take a different turn.

28.

The rows of corn
were long and straight
Every seedling, it seemed,
      had made its way
through the earth

It pained the farmer
to do the thinning
But some plants had to go
      to insure the hardy fruition
of the others

And so it is with our choices.

29.

Appetites
    Power
    Money
    Sex
    Food
Quantity does not equal satiety

The operative control is spirit —
feeling a self-worth
and an *enough-ness* within
    which is realized
through a positive expressing
rather than by possessing
    or consuming.

30.

Envy distances us
from that which we would be or have
Admiration allows access

And envy can grow
        into admiration
as our perspective is adjusted
from self-condemnation
        to self-approval.

31.

A hard, unyielding attitude
       (a facet of fear)
is a repellent
to the love
       who wants to come near.

32.

A child
  abused
  neglected
  or unloved
feels unprotected and afraid

For how many years
  does this search
for security and approval
hinder one's peace
  with himself and others
And how long and arduous is the journey
to come to the affective realization
  of the reason
and the resolution.

33.

If I were given sight to see
what's inside you — and you could see
what's inside me
how do you think our world would be

If love and soul
were all that showed
and if our hearts would learn to know
how to heal where hurt has been
ah, how much our Self would grow

Speaking love
and hope and care
seeking only what we'd share
giving that
which we would have
inflicting only what we'd bear.

34.

A bird could sit forever
      if he didn't try his wings
Would never know the joy of flight
never feel what makes him sing.

35.

Another may help you
        become aware of
and use more effectively
your potential

But he cannot add
to what you are.

36.

Our ideal is our Real
and our Destination
We are enroute to that
    which our Being sees

Our dreams
speak clues to the Direction
and experience provides materials
    for use on our journey
None is extraneous.

37.

Pain
denied and rejected
becomes disguised as
    anger
    fear
    mistrust
    or physical distress
and only delays the integration
of that which would work toward
its healing.

38.

Criticism by you
of your own vulnerable points
hinders their growing
        into that which would add
strength and depth

Those vulnerabilities
look to you for acceptance
        not based on performance
and for confidence
in what they will become.

39.

Unresolved anger
        becomes as a hearty weed
choking out the growth
of those tender shoots
        which produce
the fruits of the spirit.

Understanding, accepting love
        applied to the roots
withers the weed.

40.

When hurt is felt,
assigning blame
      does not lessen the pain
It only extends it to others.

41.

What can melt the anger
which now besets my soul
what can turn it into love —
that pain from seeds I did not sow

Ah, yes, I see what put it there
hurt from long ago
and the pain I know when I feel it
seems only to make it grow

They didn't know how my soul was hurt
when it seemed that no one heard
I learned to keep my thoughts within
and didn't share in words

The hurt turned into anger
that started keeping people out
building a wall without a gate
not allowing *my* getting out

But Love found a way to scale the wall
and say there was a way
it would show me if I'd follow
and learn what it had to say

But, said Love, I couldn't walk
the way that it had come
      (we must go *through* the wall)
and it found a crack, though tiny,
and made a narrow hall

To go the way that Love would say
I must get very small
I'd almost have to disappear
to get through that narrow hall

But, said Love, *that* part of me
didn't have a size at all
that I would never lose me
by seeming very small

To get out to the other side
I'd have to leave some parts behind
but nothing that I would ever need
to know a peace of mind

I will change the Past, said Love
you'll learn to see it through my eyes
and by our walking together
that will give us time

Believe you'll see the other side
it's better far than you might think
and you will know I'm here beside you
even when there's pain

So close we'll be that I'll become
an ever-present part of you
that part which always helps you know
whatever thing is true

Just know my way takes learning
and always there is more
to help you grow, to help you know
the special soul you are.

42.

There's time for the learning

Piecing together and blending
        the parts of you
is the process of becoming

The darkness of some parts
need never frighten
They only express their need
        for your caring
and direction
Your acknowledgment and understanding
provide the light they seek.

43.

Reaching out to unknown realms
where we've not been before
can make us feel uncertain
until we reach the other shore

The voyage will have some doubting times
we'll think sometimes of turning back
to that we know—familiar roads
Yes, there's the choice of turning back

But think—just why the journey
remember its reason well
it needs be that which speaks the soul
Retreat? Only our soul can tell

We must heed no other voices
our soul alone has leave to speak
and if our soul has planned the voyage
we will reach the shore we seek.

44.

The goal is not to *change*
but to *Be*
for Being is the source
of all growth
and speaks our connected-ness
to that Essence
of which we are a part

Being
is a stillness and a positive power
non-threatening
and feeling no threat
because it is an All-ness.

45.

He who attempts
to live with certainty
is like unto one
 who would deny
the flow of a river.

46.

To know there's a purpose
in who you are
and in what your life will speak
can strengthen
　　　many a weary day
when it *feels* it may never be

Yes, the purpose is firm
and a certainty
It's built inside
where the spirit sees

　　　But it may take time
　　　for the outside to know
　　　your reason for being
　　　that's known by the soul.

the light is within

47.

That Spirit within
      is like unto a traveler
sent from another world
to guide me through this one

It goes where'er
      I take it
It feels my joy
and it will suffer
      what I suffer
But it will not leave

As I recognize its presence
      and give it voice
it will teach me
all I ever need know.

48.

A seed lies waiting
deep inside
to speak the self
you want to "find"

Just help it grow
the best you know
by sharing love
      that *now* you know.

49.

My Center
is my sense of Self
It is that which rights my vessel
   on a stormy sea
It is my inner eye
and it is a doorway
   allowing communion
between things temporal and spiritual
It is the source of my strength
and allows my acceptance of matters
   beyond my understanding
until Time and Love shall speak
their meaning to me

Times there are
when the flood of events and emotions
may seem to dislodge
   or obscure that Center
But the clearing of the debris
will show that
it is my indestructible Eternal.

50.

That balance of action
and some time for *not doing*
allows for the emergence
　　　of that intuition
from our soul
which most clearly speaks
　　　our Self

Learning ways to best listen
and to speak that message
　　　through our living
is our primary purpose.

51.

Condemnation
doesn't encourage me
     to grow
Caring does

And I must believe
that a spirit
     strong
     deep
     and gentle
is the Source
from which I draw
and is that which impels
rather than compels
     my growing toward it
as a plant reaches toward the light.

52.

Speak, my soul,
and say to me
things that you have learned
Speak the wisdom
that is you
speak the love that you have learned

Speak the comfort
that I need
when I'm lonely and alone
Say to me
that love's still here
when I feel it's gone

Speak and stir my memory
of all that love can be
Speak and speak
and speak and speak
Heal my misery.

53.

A warm little light
at the end of the hall
helps me feel
        not scared at all

It watches o'er the dark,
you see,
until I learn
I need not be
        scared at all
when Love's with me.

54.

When your resources feel spent
and your spirit exhausted
let not this be a reason
    for ending your journey

Look, rather, for a resting place
    a wood
    a cathedral
    or some place of solitude
where the soul may commune with its Source
and be reminded
    that its pain is heard
and is being attended.

55.

Truth and Love
most often speak softly and gently
to introduce themselves

So there needs be
        a stillness in the soul
that they may be heard.

56.

The tears and fears of yesternight
may come again, it's true
    and yet I know
    that *all* I feel
my soul, is part of you

Not just the sunny days of hope
that light the darkened way
    not just the love
    I reach for
but *all* of life, you say

And I can trust your knowledge
as I learn to listen well
    so many truths
    so many joys
I know you want to tell

Patience, patience, oh, my Soul,
I pray you'll grant to me
    to walk whatever
    way you show
as you teach me how to see.

57.

What your soul can hear
it has the capacity
    to demonstrate.

58.

You're on your way to freedom
you're learning who you are
new ways to be — new ways to see
and peace is not afar

The past
is getting left there
by *feeling* what it was
    It cannot hold
    what you let go
as love absorbs the cause

A new sun
is arising
that gives the past new light
a brighter day
a better way
as love arights your sight.

59.

Before an egg
      can become a chick
a certain period of warmth
must be provided

Love felt and expressed
      is that warmth
needed by our spirit
for its birthing.

60.

Still the doubts
oh, my Soul,
which fear would speak
of things not yet seen
        by my eyes
Grant me confidence
that my yearnings
        foretell thy gifts

Speak patience
        to my understanding
for the unfolding of my future
as your wisdom directs.